MICKEY MANTLE

MICKEY MANTLE

An Appreciation

by MICKEY HERSKOWITZ

William Morrow and Company, Inc.
New York

It is the policy of William Morrow and Company, Inc., and
its imprints and affiliates, recognizing the importance of pre-
serving what has been written, to print the books we publish
on acid-free paper, and we exert our best efforts to that end.

Library of Congress Cataloging-in-Publication Data has been
applied for.

ISBN 0-688-14699-6

Printed in the United States of America

First Edition

1 2 3 4 5 6 7 8 9 10

BOOK DESIGN BY INTERROBANG DESIGN STUDIO

ACKNOWLEDGMENTS

Some of the moments in these pages were private ones between Mickey Mantle and the author. But many talented writers, and sportscasters, told stories and expressed sentiments that are reflected here. They include Harold Rosenthal, an old friend and one of the first to follow the Yankees' rookie sensation in the spring of 1951, Robert Lipsyte, George Vecsey, Bob Costas, and Roy Firestone.

Personal thanks are also owed to several of Mickey's former teammates, especially Tony Kubek, Whitey Ford, and Yogi Berra.

For their help and encouragement, the author is indebted to Paul Bresnick, a calm and reassuring influence, as good editors always are; to Bill Adler, whose mind is always turning, and to Jon Moskowitz, Deborah Weiss Geline, and Julie Rosner, for deflecting the usual pressures.

Many of the scenes described here were reproduced from the author's notes and memory. Other quotes are from the collections of the Society for American Baseball Research (SABR) and Paul Dickson's comprehensive work, *Baseball's Greatest Quotations*.

To a generation of young baseball fans who understood the joy Mickey Mantle brought to a game children play

"Yesterday—when I was young, the taste of life was sweet as rain upon my tongue. . . .

"I lived by night and shunned the naked light of day and only now I see how the years ran away.

"So many drinking songs were waiting to be sung. So many wayward pleasures lay in store for me, and so much pain my dazzled eyes refused to see.

"I ran so fast that time and youth at last ran out. I never stopped to think what life was all about. . . .

"There are so many songs in me that won't be sung. I feel the bitter taste of tears upon my tongue,

"The time has come to pay for Yesterday, when I was young—"

—SUNG BY ROY CLARK ON AUGUST 13, 1995,
IN DALLAS, TEXAS

*D*on't cry for Mickey Mantle. He never cried for himself.

Losing might have made him cry, at least once, when it was the World Series and the Yankees were the better team. Of course, he shed tears over the deaths of those closest to him—his father, his son Billy, and his son's namesake, Billy Martin. But he didn't always shed them when they might have helped him most, and he never wept for himself.

Right to the end, he remained an immense presence to anyone who recalled him as baseball's first great coast-to-coast TV star. His stats do not tell you who he is—not his 536 career homers, his Triple Crown in 1956, his three Most Valuable Player awards. But, mercy, what memories he must have had to warm him through the winter nights.

> *I was sitting here the other day, and I tried to remember what it was like to hit a home run and win a game. And I couldn't remember. It was like the whole thing happened to somebody else.*
>
> —MANTLE, ON HIS FIFTIETH BIRTHDAY

When he died of cancer in August 1995, the news coverage was the kind you expect to be given not to a ballplayer but to a former head of state, a de Gaulle or Churchill. There was a death watch, headlines on front pages all across America, specials on television, hourly bulletins on radio.

People gathered in their homes to talk about him.

Mantle was the last in a line of almost mythical New York Yankee sluggers who rose above their numbers and beyond the Hall of Fame: Babe Ruth, Lou Gehrig, Joe DiMaggio. He may have been the last true star who was not identified by the money he made—he was paid $100,000 in each of his last seven seasons. His fame, his legend, his popularity, seemed to rest not so much on what he achieved—and that was considerable—but on what he promised: a thrill with every at bat, power, speed, and the poetry of youth.

He never wanted to be a role model, but could not avoid being a hero. He was both at the moment of his death in a Dallas hospital, two months after the nation became aware he was battling for his life. He lost the battle an hour or two after midnight, with his wife, Merlyn, and his son David at his bedside. He was sixty-three, the once boyish face gaunt and finally revealing his age and his pain.

It would be a disservice to remember Mantle as one who drank himself to death, an absentee husband and father, a fellow who rained on his own parade. These were impressions left by the inevitable stories that made him seem sad and lost. But make no mistake. Mantle had a rich life, with an abundance of friends and merriment, more than he thought he deserved. He did not lack reasons to live. His glass was rarely half empty.

The wonder is that he functioned as well as he did, so little touched for so long by gossip or scandal. Few of his fans knew, or cared, that he drank too much, until he confronted the problem and made it public. Almost no one outside his inner circle knew that he and Merlyn lived apart for their last seven years, not even in Dallas, where he sometimes had more privacy than he really wanted.

He rode the wave of his emotions, feeling one day doomed, the next blessed with extraordinary luck. He wore Number 7, didn't he? And he was acutely conscious of the unfairness of life. He was given a break his own father, Elvin ("Mutt") Mantle, had been denied—to get paid for playing ball. He felt almost guilty that the game took him to New York and to the shrine, Yankee Stadium, while Henry Aaron was kind of buried in Milwaukee and Atlanta.

Until his liver transplant turned into a moral issue, the deepest controversy Mantle had been involved in was his suspension from baseball, along with Willie Mays, for taking a public relations job with an Atlantic City hotel. When a new liver became available forty-eight hours after Mickey went on the waiting list, accusations of special treatment flew. He was angered and troubled by them; he had never asked for special favors in his life.

His pride flared, but even the sick Mantle had enough funny bone left to chuckle at the dippy efforts of the press to absorb the medical data. At the press conference after his transplant, one of the doctors was asked, "Is the organ donor still living?"

The doctor looked at him, deadpan, and said politely, "You're a sportswriter, aren't you?"

In what turned out to be his last seventeen months, when he was cold sober, his family and teammates rallied around him. They always had. "He never changed," said Yogi Berra. "He was always just Mick. When I called the hospital, and finally got through, they said he was telling bedpan jokes to the nurses."

And almost immediately around the country, the process of explaining him began. Exactly what was it that made him Mickey Mantle, a symbol of something so vital in our lives, a song that still sang to us twenty-seven years after he played his last game? What made the connection to the rest of us so strong and so lasting?

◆　◆　◆

The quick and easy explanation is this: He was a hero at a time when we still believed in them, heroes who were all good with no bad in them. Mantle, though, was a hero who was vulnerable, whose flaws reminded us he was mortal, although it wasn't until much later that we realized how vulnerable he was, outside the lines. On the field, he failed just often enough to keep the fans from having to hate him. He came along just as television began to embrace all of sport, and he was the first made-for-TV home run hitter.

Most of all, he had the look: blond hair, blue eyes, and freckles, a big, easy smile, an Oklahoma drawl, and a walk that was just short of a swagger. He was every mother's son.

And when he took his last, sober breath, a great big chunk of the national pastime—a quaint phrase, that—went with him. Money, great, big, indecent gobs of money, have changed the dynamics of the game. It is going to be rare for a player to last twenty years, or to spend them with one team. (Cal Ripken, the Iron Bird of Baltimore, will be an exception.) The clubs pay megamillions to the superstars—an elastic phrase, that—then trade them or cut them as they age and slip. The fans will learn to guard their hearts because they can't afford to give them to a player who may not be around after three or four years.

*I hated getting hurt. That's why I hated going to doctors.
I didn't want to see them because I didn't want to
know what they would tell me.*
—MANTLE, IN A CONVERSATION

Even as the final scenes unfolded in Dallas—the appeal for an organ donor, the questions of special treatment, the successful surgery, followed by the shattering news of his cancer—the marketing of a legend continued. There were stories speculating on how much his trading cards, or an autographed ball, would be worth if he didn't survive. Even Mantle joked about it at a press conference, when he spotted a friend in the back of the room, a collector. "Hey, Barry," he needled, "did you try to buy my liver?"

This was typical Mantle wit, clubhouse humor, which always had a trace of gallows humor.

He joked about his knees, his surgical scars, his pain, which was with him daily from the mid-1950s on. He didn't mind when Whitey Ford turned those ailing legs into a running gag, using a stand-in for Mantle. Bill Kane, who kept the team's stats, bore a slight resemblance to Mickey, especially under the dim lights of a bar.

When he was with Whitey, fans jumped to the obvious conclusion and asked Kane—as Mick—for his autograph. He would go through the ritual of identifying himself, politely insisting he wasn't Mantle.

At that point, Ford would pipe up, "Aw, go ahead, Mick, sign for the guy." Often, to avoid spending the night arguing the point, Kane would sign. Sooner or later, the fan would ask how his legs were, and this gave Whitey his next cue. "Come on, Mick," he would say, "show the guy your legs."

It happened that Bill Kane had overcome a bout of polio as a child, but one of his legs was considerably thinner than the other. Ford would prompt him until Kane raised his trouser leg, assuring the stranger that "this one isn't so bad. It's coming along."

The stranger would stare at the leg, tip his glass to "Mantle" and his guts, and hurry away. Ford would tell the story to Mick the next day, and the two of them would howl with laughter.

Of course, Mantle didn't need a designated leg to prove his courage. Early Wynn, who never in his life had expressed sympathy for a hitter, watched him change into his uniform before an All-Star game: "I watched him bandage that knee—that whole leg—and I saw what he had to go through every day to play. He was taped from shin to thigh. And now I'll never be able to say enough in praise. Seeing those legs, his power becomes unbelievable."

For the most part, Mantle accepted his injuries as part of the cost of doing business. Very rarely, the constant references made him defensive. "They keep talking about me getting hurt," he said. "I still played eighteen years. I played in more games than anyone else in Yankee history."

Although others made the excuse for him, Mantle tried to avoid any suggestion that the drinking was a sedative for his injuries. Some of his teammates said he was too strong for the game, another way of saying he demanded too much of his body. He was a remarkable specimen, listed as a half inch under six feet tall. By 1961, he weighed 210 pounds and the team doctor said that he had almost zero body fat.

He was a blend of brawn and baseball history, the third dimension in a Willard Mullin cartoon: shoulders three columns wide, his waist one column, his bat half a page long, and Number 7 a giant exclamation point on a pinstriped field. Part of what drove him was his sense of the past. He was always a marquee figure in out-of-town stadiums, where in the normal course of events the Yankees would be leading the league by nineteen games in August, and Ruth, Gehrig, DiMaggio, or Mantle would squash the home team twice on a hot Sunday afternoon.

Dr. Sidney Gaynor compared his muscles to the fictional Popeye's, but all of his joints—wrists, knees, ankles—were frail. His muscles, the doctor explained, were too strong for his bones, and he paid a price in torn ligaments and cartilage.

The forgotten part of Mantle's game was his baserunning. He had a career total of 153 stolen bases, an average of less than ten a year. He might have set records, but he had no license to steal. The unwritten rule allowed him to take off only if the Yankees were tied or in a one-run game.

The whole bench flinched whenever Mickey had to slide.

Of course, the Yankees of his era played for the long ball and the big inning. The stolen base wasn't a part of their tradition, as it was with the old Dodgers.

> *I saw Duke Snider at a card show, and he came up and whispered in my ear, "Hey, Mantle, these golden years really suck, don't they?" But, you know, when I retired I got more than fifty scrapbooks people sent me in the mail. It gave me goose bumps to know I had that kind of effect on people. Billy Crystal did a sketch for* Saturday Night Live, *and they ran it again on* This Week in Baseball. *He's talking about how his dad took him to a game one time, and then he says, "Mick hit one out of the park. It was a good day." That's nice, really nice, to have people feel that way.*
>
> —MANTLE, IN A CONVERSATION, 1994

The sports collectors' industry renewed and enlarged Mantle's celebrity. He was the player most sought. There was no mystery to him, as there was with DiMaggio, who, after all, was once married to Marilyn Monroe. "Mantle is the one people remember," said one authority, "the one who has bridged the generations."

Babe Ruth was lionized and Joe DiMaggio was revered. Ted Williams gave us hitting as a science. Willie Mays showed us the joy and Hank Aaron the grace. But for Mantle there was a feeling close to love. He was the best player on the best team of his era, he brought the crowd to its feet for eighteen years and hit 536 home runs, broke records, made it to the Hall of Fame. Did anyone ever accomplish so much and leave us begging for more? He asked it of himself: How much more could he have done on sound legs and with healthier habits? He never stopped asking. No one was harder on him than Mick himself.

He would argue with strangers who had said something as simple as "Mick, you're the greatest."

"No," I heard him respond, after signing over eight hundred books in two hours, going through them like a corn-husking machine. Then he launched into a short lecture: "You have to look at the records, and when you do that you have to say that I didn't have the career Willie Mays had. He played a lot longer and did a lot more. The guys who took good care of themselves, like Willie and Stan Musial and Hank Aaron and Pete Rose, they're the ones who put up the big numbers."

Always, he found it hard to accept a compliment and often he would hide behind a quip.

I've often thought that a lot of awards you get are made-up deals so you'll come to the dinners.

—MANTLE, 1985

He blamed his lifestyle, his thirst, his casual approach to conditioning, for any shortages in his career. He was arguably the biggest talent of his time, the fastest runner the game had known going from home to first base, batting left-handed. No one hit a ball farther from both sides of the plate. Few covered as much ground in centerfield.

He played the game the way little kids did in their dreams. And he came to represent the dominance of the Yankees, playing in twelve World Series in his first fourteen years, breaking Babe Ruth's record for home runs in the fall classic (with eighteen). "There has never been anyone like this kid," manager Casey Stengel said when Mantle was a rookie. "He has more speed than any slugger, and more slug than any speedster."

It is hard to imagine a time when we didn't know him. Old men knew him. Little kids knew him. Even educated ladies knew him. Great player. Bad knees. A Huck Finn face. (This might be the place to mention that Mantle never had a fight in his entire baseball career. The closest he came was during his rookie season, when a pitcher threw a fastball that he judged too close to his chin. He glared out at the mound, and the pitcher yelled to him, "What's the matter with you, Huckface?" Mick thought the description started with the letter "F" but the catcher corrected him. Years later, he said he didn't charge the mound because he never did figure out what the pitcher meant.)

Mickey Mantle. The name brushes the lips like a feather. You try to picture him at nineteen, with short hair, his usual wardrobe consisting of a white T-shirt and blue jeans, reporting to the Yankees in the spring of 1951 wearing his only sports coat, the sleeves barely reaching his wrists.

In the winter before that season, he was just another pretty face in the Yankees' prosperous farm system, a kid whose name the writers could drop into their hot-stove league stories.

Harold Rosenthal, a kindly, diligent veteran who covered New York teams for the *Herald Tribune*, dropped Mickey a note as he routinely did to the team's emerging prospects. In it, he requested certain basic information that could be used, or not, as events would decide.

Mickey had hit .383 in Class C ball in Joplin, enough to catch the eye of the front office—and any beat writer looking for a comer, or a sleeper, a name to slip into an off-season yarn.

Even then, when good manners were more in fashion and people had lots of time to fill, the chances were less than fifty-fifty that the writer would receive a reply. But a letter with an Oklahoma postmark reached Rosenthal promptly. It was written on paper from a dime-store notepad, yellow and lined.

The note was friendly and as informative as one might hope from an untraveled nineteen-year-old. "He said that Phil Rizzuto was his idol," recalled

Rosenthal, "and that he had committed seventy errors as a shortstop." (Actually, that figure was also an error. Mantle had been charged with fifty-five errors, an indication that Mickey was hard on himself even then. Still, the number was enough to convince his manager in Joplin, Harry Craft, that his future was not at shortstop.)

The letter was printed, rather than written in longhand. In it, he mentioned getting kicked in the leg while playing high school football, and the treatment that followed for osteomyelitis. The teenager did not go into any of the details, but the injury would keep him out of the Army during the Korean War. It also helped explain why he was such a slow healer for all of his career.

He closed by adding that he had twin brothers, Roy and Ray, who would be even better athletes than he was. In fact, they did sign with the Yankees but never made it past Class A ball.

◆   ◆   ◆

What do ya think, I was born old?

—CASEY STENGEL TO AN ASTONISHED MANTLE,

SHOWING HIM HOW HE USED TO PLAY THE

RIGHT FIELD WALL IN EBBETS FIELD

Although Casey Stengel is usually given the credit for converting Mantle into an outfielder, it was Harry Craft who first tried him there. "He was just a baby," said Harry, "with freckles all over his face. But in Joplin he hit twenty-six homers, fourteen left-handed, twelve right, and they went over buildings."

It was clear to Craft, and soon to Stengel, that the Yankees would need to replace DiMaggio long before Rizzuto had spent himself at short. Craft had been a centerfielder with the Reds, one of the best of his time. In his reports to New York, he kept telling them that they needed to play Mickey in the outfield to take advantage of his speed. And he had an awful weakness for a shortstop—he kept muffing the easy play, the ball hit right at him.

Craft later managed two teams in the majors, in Kansas City and Houston. It was in Kansas City, in 1959, that he saw the potential in a young fellow named Roger Maris. When the A's fired him after the season, he saw Stengel at the World Series and urged him to sign Maris.

His raw talent propelled Mantle in baseball, but he was even less seasoned socially. He stayed to himself in Joplin, and had a habit of not looking people in the eye when they talked to him. He was mortified when his roommate made a pass at an attractive brunette, an "older" woman of maybe twenty-eight or thirty, in a diner. She turned out to be their manager's lady friend, and the next day Craft called a team meeting and laid down two rules that Mantle never forgot: "If you want to stay in baseball, you don't eat where the manager eats. You don't drink where the manager drinks. If you walk into a place and he's at a table, you say hello and you walk out." And the next time any player made a move on one of his babes, Harry said, he would kick their ass. Mantle kept his head down until Craft finished talking.

Harry was a handsome man, who at the time was between wives. He had a quiet strength that Mantle admired. It was a quality his father had. So did DiMaggio and Ralph Houk and Hank Bauer. It wasn't a quality he looked for in his friends, but he found it in the people he often wanted to copy.

Harry Craft died on August 3, 1995, at the age of eighty. A day later, Mantle reentered the hospital in Dallas for his final stay.

When I was twenty years old, I was a better ballplayer than [in my prime]. I could hit better, run faster, and throw better. Yet they farmed me out to the minor leagues. I was too young to take all the pressures of major league ball. When a boy of

> *twenty can handle it, you've got yourself a real*
> *special ballplayer—a Williams, a Musial, or a*
> *Cobb.*
>
> —MANTLE, 1961

The young Mantle was an intriguing mixture, part James Dean and part Li'l Abner. He was shy, sensitive, sometimes sullen or coarse, strong and yet gentle, with a temper and playfulness that were both close to the surface. "He was strong as a mule," Whitey Ford once joked, "and just as smart."

It was a portrait he never completely outgrew. Nor is there much evidence that he felt a need to do so. He was what he was, and this consistency was part of what his friends and fans trusted most. Of course, he changed in material ways. He enjoyed fine foods and custom-tailored clothes and high-powered cars. His soft blond hair was blow-dried and styled. But his attitude was still down-home and his looks never came across as glossy.

I once stood behind a mature woman in a drug-store who picked up a magazine with a twenty-four-year-old Mantle on the cover. "That," she said, "is a beautiful face."

The little boy that lurked inside, always waiting for a chance to pop out of Mantle's skin, expressed himself in assorted ways. One of them was in his unending desire to pitch an inning in a Yankee game. He wanted to show off a knuckleball that he simply discovered one day he could throw, part of his arsenal of natural athletic talent.

From all accounts, including his own, the knuckler was a beauty. "Mickey's pitch," observed Tony Kubek, "was unhittable. It was uncatchable." He would show it to Whitey Ford and gloat, "This is something you don't have."

He kept begging Casey Stengel to let him pitch, anytime a game was well out of reach. Casey was tempted because if he shared anything with Mantle, it was a tolerance for the absurd.

After a while, none of the catchers would warm

up with Mantle—not Berra or Elston Howard or John Blanchard. Mickey was reduced to having to use rookies. The Yankees had signed Jake Gibbs, an all-American quarterback at Ole Miss, and brought him to the stadium to work out. Mantle invited him to play catch. Gibbs was thrilled.

After lobbing a few soft knuckleballs, Mickey said, "I'm warmed up now, so maybe you better put on a catcher's mask." Gibbs didn't think he needed one.

Kubek remembers the scene: "Mickey sighed and said okay. Then he uncorked a knuckler that took off and then we heard this *splat*. That was Jake's nose and it was all over his face. Mickey broke more than one nose with that knuckler."

Stengel finally ordered him to quit throwing the pitch, in the belief that it may have aggravated a shoulder that had been bothering him. Later, Ralph Houk listened to his plea to pitch, but quickly dismissed the idea. Houk didn't want to show up the other team, and he didn't want to

risk hurting his franchise player. But his teammates would sit on the bench and speculate about
what would happen if Mantle got into a game,
and if he could get the knuckler over the plate,
could anyone hit it? (Some twenty-plus years later,
the muscular Jose Canseco talked his manager into
letting him pitch an inning of a lost cause for the
Texas Rangers. Canseco tore up his shoulder and
was useless the rest of the season.)

A team is where a boy can prove his courage on his own.
A gang is where a coward goes to hide.
—MANTLE, WIDELY QUOTED

Those were not Mickey's words. Someone
wrote them for him to deliver at a banquet. He
was not a clever phrasemaker, did not speak in
epigrams, but certainly would have endorsed the
sentiment of the words. As the years vanished from
his screen, he felt an almost urgent need to repay

his debt to baseball and to the kids who were his uncritical supporters. He had found his theme as he recovered from his own alcohol abuse: Don't drink or do drugs. He gave the message a more intense twist at the dramatic press conference on July 11 at the Baylor University Medical Center.

He had lost forty pounds after his surgery, and his appearance was a shock. He wore a baseball cap that seemed too large for his head. He said he felt shaky and nervous, but his words were almost jaunty: "If you're looking for a role model, this is it. Don't be like me." He motioned toward himself with his thumb.

Nothing he said was out of character. For all his years, he was committed to a clear and rigid personal code. He would not be boastful. Showing up an opponent, taunting anyone, were acts that he regarded as obscene. Always, he put the team first. His teammates knew this and the fans sensed it.

If Mantle ever stood at home plate for more than a nanosecond and followed the flight of a ball, it was because he misjudged his swing and didn't realize he had hit one out. He rounded the bases with his head down, his gait normal. If he couldn't conceal a grin, he at least contained it until he crossed the plate, or made his way past the backslaps and onto the bench.

Mantle and Ford were always mindful of the gap between their salaries and a Moose Skowron, an Elston Howard, a Tony Kubek. They collected the checks they received from certain endorsements, five hundred dollars here and a thousand there, and didn't take them home. Instead, they tucked them into the box reserved for valuables in the clubhouse. When eight or ten grand had accumulated, they threw a dinner party for the entire team, wives included, with steaks and drinks and a floor show.

Ford was in the Army during Mantle's rookie year, and he was married in Astoria on a day when the Yankees played an exhibition game against the Dodgers at Ebbets Field. The bride's family had sent a routine invitation to the ball club, not expecting a response. But Stengel, in one of his whims, piled the entire team into a bus after the game and had the driver take them to the wedding reception.

Nearly everyone went inside, but Mantle, feeling awkward and out of place, stayed in his seat on the almost empty bus. After the reception, the newly married couple came aboard to say thanks and shake hands. One of the hands belonged to Mickey, and that was how they met, Mantle and Ford. "I remember thinking," said Whitey, "what a hayseed."

During my eighteen years I came to bat almost ten thousand times. I struck out about one thousand seven hundred times and walked maybe one thousand eight hundred times. You figure a ballplayer will average about five hundred at bats a season. That means I played seven years without ever hitting the ball.

—MICKEY MANTLE, LOOKING BACK ON

HIS CAREER

His popularity lasted, and even increased, because he was perceived as humble, and when that wore off he was admired for being human, a star haunted by injury and tempted by bright lights. To fans in the 1950s and 1960s, his imperfections were seen as harmless and his talent as Olympian. So he broke a few curfews, partied too hard, invested too eagerly, and gave the press less than it wanted.

But he never bragged, never struck poses, never pretended that he viewed the game with the mind of a chemist.

Yogi Berra once told me about Mantle taking a seat beside him, in the late innings of a game, before his next turn at bat. "What's this guy got?" he asked, nodding at the pitcher.

Berra's neck swiveled. "Mick," he said, "you've already hit against him three times. The guy has been in the league five years."

"Aw, you know me," said Mantle with a sheepish grin. "I'm just up there swingin'." He turned toward the dugout steps. On the first pitch, he doubled off the wall.

> *No man in the history of baseball had as much power as Mickey Mantle. No man. You're not talking about ordinary power. Dave Kingman had power. Willie Mays had power. Then when you're talking about Mantle—it's an altogether different level.*
>
> —BILLY MARTIN

No one ever questioned Mickey Mantle's pride or self-honesty. He reacted tartly when Reggie Jackson passed him on the all-time home run list, and a wire service reporter called him for a reaction. "He passed me on the all-time strikeout list a couple of years ago," he snapped, "and nobody asked me about that."

He heard the same questions so often for so many years that, in self-defense, he developed a set of stock answers. He was the first male in his family to live past the age of forty-one, and he turned his survival into a quip: "If I had known I was gonna live this long, I'd have taken better care of myself." The truth was his final irony.

He did not cast a wide net in choosing friends, but they came to him easily and there was very little turnover. Membership was by invitation only. The list consisted mainly of his former teammates, his golfing buddies, and those who conducted his business, won his trust, and kept his secrets. You couldn't qualify by taking a number and standing in line.

He had a status that was rare, even irregular, because his friends protected him, at times made excuses for him, and still saw him as special. Knowing him, liking him, did not entitle you to any claim on his friendship. I helped him with a book about his World Series experiences, *All My Octobers,* and saw the physical pain and the emotional turmoil. I don't know if that made us friends. We got along well—partly because of some very sound advice I was offered.

That advice came from Kathy Hampton, who was the administrator for the firm of Roy True, Mantle's lawyer and longtime friend. She said not to push him. He got turned off by writers, or anyone else, who wanted to be his new best friend, who got in the habit of calling too often or hanging around when they hadn't been asked.

I was also told that interviews should be held no later than eleven in the morning, and I should not expect to reach Mick at night. Afternoons were reserved for golf. There was a hint in this instruction that I missed. I did not yet know about the seriousness of the drinking, the "Breakfast of Champions" in the morning—Kahlúa, brandy, and cream—or the four to five glasses of wine for lunch, the vodka dinners.

I did not find it hard to respect his space. He was, after all, Mickey Mantle and he had earned the right to pick his own friends. I limited my calls and kept them brief. When we met, if he asked me to turn off the tape recorder, I did, recognizing it as a signal that what he wanted to say was off the record. If he started to fidget, I cut the interviews short.

I watched him drink, but can't say that I ever saw him drunk. He was not an angry drinker, he did not turn physical and start looking for an argument. His laugh got louder, his jokes cruder, but if he seemed anything, it was content—to stay put, whooping it up with his pals. "It amazed me sometimes," he said, "how much liquor I could hold."

His final days, indeed his final year and a half, would be crowded with irony. In January 1994, he attracted a wave of national support when he made public his decision to seek treatment for a "forty-year-old" drinking problem, one that began in his prime as a Yankee and worsened in his years away from the game.

A doctor, one of his golfing companions, studied his face on the golf course one day, and saw something behind the bloodshot eyes and the yellowish skin. He told Mantle bluntly that his next drink "might be your last." A physical exam the next morning confirmed what the doctor suspected—Mantle's red blood cell count was at dangerously low levels. He had to cancel an operation that had been planned to replace one or both knees.

Mick entered The Betty Ford Center, went through rehab, and swore to stay sober. His friends told him he looked ten years younger. He was trimmer and sharper. He kept his vow, but no one knew yet that he had turned the page too late;

the damage to his system could not be reversed. He had less than a year and a half left of his wholesome new life.

A couple of weeks before he was to begin promoting his book, he told me in a phone call that he dreaded the trip. He didn't have to say why. He knew what most of the questions would be. I offered to fly to New York for the start of the tour, if he thought I might be of any help.

"Yeah, if you could stay a few days, I'd like that," Mantle said. There was a distinct pause and then he added, "But, you know . . . I don't drink anymore."

I started to crack a joke, but then I realized what he was trying to tell me. He wasn't sure he would be fun to be around anymore, now that he was sober. I said, "Mick, I'm no drinker. One glass of wine is about my limit. I'll keep you company. We can live it up on diet Sprite."

We checked into the Regency Hotel the week, as it happened, that the Houston Rockets were playing the Knicks in the NBA finals. I had just started working on a column for my newspaper when the phone rang. Mantle said he was going over to his restaurant and invited me to join him for dinner. I silently cursed my timing and told him I was sorry, I had some writing to finish. I second-guessed myself most of the night. It would have been nice to enjoy dinner with Mantle, and help celebrate his resignation from the liquor industry. But, at least, he knew that I wasn't one of those writers who sticks to you like a tick and has to be burned out with a hot match.

Then, damned if the same thing didn't happen the next night. Except that this time the Rockets and the Knicks were playing at Madison Square Garden, and I was leaving to cover the game. "Have you got a girl in there?" he asked, half

teasing and half suspicious. "No, just a computer."
I offered to get him tickets if he wanted to catch
the action. "Naw," said Mantle. "I'll watch it on
the big screen. I can't handle those concrete steps
at the Garden."

It dawned on me that he would not want to
risk having people see him stumble or fall. Meanwhile, I missed two chances to have dinner with
the Mick. There would be other chances to talk,
of course, but I felt like a nerd. In the press room,
the main course was beef and noodles on a Sty-
rofoam plate.

*The thing I miss the most is the clubhouse. Not the way
I played the last four years—that wasn't fun.
[But] I've got some guys on this team that are
almost like brothers to me—Pepi, Tresh, Stottle-
myre. I'm probably their biggest fan. First thing I
do every morning is pick up the paper and see how
they did.*

—MANTLE, HIS FIRST YEAR OUT OF BASEBALL

Gradually, we reached a certain level of comfort. At his fantasy camp in Fort Lauderdale, Mick was in fine form, relaxed and funny, tossing off barbs at the campers, recycling old stories with the ex-Yankees who made up his staff. The coaches included the ageless Enos Slaughter, Johnny Blanchard, Bobby Murcer, Jake Gibbs, and two of his sons, Mickey Jr. and David.

Hank Bauer didn't make it. "Hank has lung cancer," said Mantle, lowering his voice. "He's in bad shape. Doesn't look like he'll last much longer." Not quite a year later, Bauer was one of the pallbearers at Mantle's funeral.

I no longer remember what we were talking about during one of the breaks, only that Mickey startled me with a statement out of nowhere. "I've never told my sons I love them," he said.

He just tapped it out there, like a ground ball, waiting to see if I would field it. His face was blank. I suspect my face was flushed and revealed how unsettled I felt.

"Aw, Mick," I said, aware that his sons were grown men now, thirties to forties. "You have to tell them. It's certainly not too late."

"They know how I feel about them," he said. "They know I love them. I just have a hard time saying the words."

"Do it," I persisted, getting awfully close, I suspected, to a line you didn't cross with Mantle. "They need to hear it. I tell my kids I love them if we talk for five minutes on the phone, and all they wanted were tickets to a ballgame."

Mantle looked me straight in the eye, as if he were thinking deeply about what I had just said. "I have a hard time hugging my mother, too," he added.

We moved on to another subject. I had seen Mickey around his sons. They looked at him with worshipful eyes, but they had known him best as a drinking buddy, a fact that hit him hard in the last two years of his life. I resolved, once the book was out, or not long afterward, to ask Mantle if he had ever told Mickey Jr., David, and Danny, his three surviving sons, that he loved them. For a reason I can't really explain, it was important to me. And I thought it was important to him—to say the magic words.

He did not talk much about his mother, but his affection for her was not in doubt. When he was growing up, she cooked on a wooden stove and did the laundry in the backyard on a washboard and she always made it convenient for Mutt and then Mickey to play ball. But he wanted to remember her as the doting young mother she once was, pleasant-looking and strong-willed. He didn't deal easily with the passage of time or with awkward circumstances. Now Lovell Mantle was in her mid-nineties, frail and in a nursing home. I guessed that he shrank from physical contact partly out of a fear of hurting her, and partly because the Mantles were just not very demonstrative. She died a few months after his book was published.

If it occurred to Mickey, he left the thought unsaid, but there was longevity on his mother's side, Hodgkin's on his father's. The latter skipped him. He may have squandered the former.

In New York, on the day in June when he started his book tour, he appeared on two television shows, did a signing at B. Dalton on Sixth Avenue, and was interviewed by *USA Today*. When he walked out of the restaurant that bears his name, heading for a waiting limousine, an elderly woman in a cotton housedress pulled two copies of the book out of a bag and approached him.

Mantle stopped cold and turned on her. "This is the fifth or sixth time I've seen you today," he said. "You're working for those autograph dealers and I'm damned tired of it. Now get out of my face."

He slid into the backseat and told the driver to take off. The bag lady was still standing on the sidewalk, the books in her hand. There were five of us in the car, including a friend of Mantle's and a publicist for the publisher. No one spoke. Mantle sat back, his face pinched. He was in his fifth month of being sober and his body was going through unpleasant changes. His mood swings were ragged and at times you had to hang on around the curves.

We had gone about three blocks when Mickey snapped, "Take a right at this corner and go back to the restaurant." When the car pulled back up to the curb, the bag lady was still there. Mantle reached inside the pocket of his sports coat where he usually kept a couple dozen preautographed cards, with his photo on one side and lifetime record on the other. He took about half, handed them to his friend in the front seat, and said, "Go give these to her."

Then we drove off a second time, again in silence, Mantle's expression unchanged. He felt guilty for being angry and rude with an old woman who had nothing. Yet you sensed his annoyance at the thought of himself as a soft touch. The autograph industry had started to drive people nuts. Collectors were hiring people to stand in front of restaurants half a day to pick up signatures. Mantle saw the nuttiness in it, as well as the profits, and the underground market. He didn't want to think too much about it. In that instant, he looked disgusted, as if he had been solicited by drug dealers.

Even sitting still for an hour or more could be grueling for Mantle, especially as he struggled to fine-tune his new lifestyle. He was perched on a stool in a television studio, taking part in what is called a satellite feed. As many as two dozen sportscasters could plug into the line, fire off a few questions, and later air a video of what would appear to be a one-on-one interview with Mickey Mantle.

He knew this drill and he kept his humor—for most of the session. But he was edgy, moving toward testy, because the questions were piling up. At one point, an unseen voice inquired, "How did you feel when Billy died?"

I was standing in the control booth, but my eyes were riveted on Mantle. He looked as if he had been slapped in the face. His jaw dropped. One hand moved toward the microphone that had been pinned to his shirt collar.

But at that moment, the flustered sportscaster added, "I mean, you guys played together so many seasons and were so close, how did you deal with it when you heard the news?"

You could almost see the veins in Mantle's neck deflate. The question had been about Billy Martin, who had been killed when the truck he was riding in skidded off a snow-packed road on Christmas Day in 1989. The police report said the accident was drinking-related.

Mantle gave a tactful, heartfelt answer, but he was visibly relieved when the session ended.

"Man, I came that close to losing it," he said. At first, he thought the question referred to his son Billy, who had died of a heart attack in March, at thirty-six. (Billy had been named after the ex-Yankee infielder and manager.) Billy's death had been complicated by Hodgkin's disease, and a long bout with booze and prescription drugs. It was another knot in the tangled rope of Mantle's past twelve months, which also included the death of his mother and his stint at The Betty Ford Center.

"From now on," said Mickey, with a scowl, "no more questions about anybody who died."

What was lucky for me was playing in New York, with all the big TV and radio networks, the wire services, and all the magazines. Willie Mays and I, we broke in together in 1951 and then the big question was always, "Who's the best, Willie, Mick, or the Duke?" I always said, long before Henry Aaron broke Ruth's home run record, that

Hank was the best ballplayer of our era. He was doing the same thing Willie and I were doing. He just wasn't doing it in New York.

—MANTLE, IN A CONVERSATION

Getting to New York, and the launching of *All My Octobers*, had not been a cakewalk. When the manuscript was nearly finished, Mantle announced that he was voluntarily entering The Betty Ford Center, and there was a mild crisis with the publisher, HarperCollins. His announcement said he had suffered blackouts and memory loss, an admission not likely to thrill a publisher who is about to release a book based on memories that go back forty years or more.

I had to fly to New York to confer with the lawyers, and we spent the first of several days verifying names, dates, and events. In truth, he might have been vague about the exact year, but Mickey's recall of specific moments in his Yankee career, down to the ball-and-strike count, were often uncanny.

I argued that we were overreacting. The black-outs, the memory loss, I insisted, had more to do with the times he was on a binge and could not remember how he behaved or who he insulted— and might not want to remember.

Weeks later, after Mickey had returned to Dallas and was slowly reemerging, I called to discuss the book's epilogue, which dealt with the disclosure of his drinking problem. I asked if he wanted me to mail a copy to his office.

"No," he said, "send it to me here at home."

I said I didn't have that address.

"Wait a second," he said, "I'll get it for you." He turned away from the phone, and I heard his voice call out to what I presumed was the housekeeper, "Hey, Ophelia, what's the address here?"

When we hung up, I called Kathy Hampton, unsure what to conclude, but thinking Mickey might be in a clinic or a halfway house and, if so, this was something I may need to know.

I explained my reason for calling and she understood. She asked me what number I had dialed. Yes, that was the right home number. She asked what address he had given me. Yes, that was the right address.

"Oh," I said, still puzzled, "well, everything is fine then. Sorry if I raised an unnecessary alarm."

There was a pause, and as an afterthought, Kathy said, "He only moved in two and a half years ago."

I let that information sort of dangle. I have never seen a survey on how long it takes most people to memorize their addresses, but in Mantle's case, he did not let certain mundane facts clutter his mind. On the other hand, I decided the review the lawyers insisted on probably had been a good idea.

We were in Kathy's office, in Dallas, when she told us that the publisher had called to say that the week of the book's official publication date it would make its debut at number eight on *The New York Times* best-seller list. "You should be very proud of yourselves," she said.

Mantle smiled a crinkle-eyed smile, and shook his head in what I took to be an expression of amazement. He had missed much of the hassle of the book's closing, and he seemed unsure whether we should congratulate each other. He ducked his head and, still smiling, gave me a noogie on my right arm. I had heard over and over again that meeting Mantle made his fans, once boys, now in their forties or fifties, feel like schoolkids. Now I understood. This was, I thought, pure Mantle, a classic example of his nonverbal communication.

Many New York writers who had covered his deeds on an almost daily basis for eighteen years knew him far better than I ever would. He was too shy, too country, too naïve for the tastes of some of them when he first arrived. The writers, who felt pressured to have the players like them, were pleased just to have Mantle say good morning.

But he was above all a trusting soul, and continued to be—in spurts. Mantle lent his name to a series of businesses that went kaput. There were the country-cooking franchises, a men's clothing store in Atlanta, an employment agency that paired him with Joe Namath, and a bowling alley in Dallas.

"They were going to give it to Doak Walker," he recalled, "but Doak was having some kind of family problem, so they asked me to come in. It never paid off and we sold it to some people from New Jersey. I had a great slogan for the restaurants: 'The best piece of chicken you can get unless you're a rooster.' Those kind of ideas were probably what put us out of business."

He lent his name to these ventures, but invested little if any of his own money. "Yeah," he said, "but that hurts, too. Pretty soon people say, 'My God, is Mantle in it? It'll go belly up for sure.' "

He steadied himself financially around 1968, when he was trying to get out of the fast-food deal. He took the advice of a friend who referred him to Roy True, then thirty-eight and a partner in a firm specializing in corporate law. From then on, he said, "I wouldn't walk around the corner to a Little League banquet if Roy didn't tell me it was okay."

Money was important to Mick, but it never consumed him, and he tipped big and spent freely. True steered him to large, substantial companies such as Allied Chemical and Fuji Photo. He began picking up nice fees for appearances and golf outings. Roy was selective, turning down about 90 percent of the requests that kept pouring in.

Unlike Joe DiMaggio, Mantle had never gone away. He just moved (in 1966) to Dallas, where he and Merlyn lived in the same house for more than twenty years. In the winter, people would spot him and ask if he was in town for a banquet. They assumed that Mickey Mantle had to live in New York, probably on Park Avenue. But Dallas was where Merlyn wanted to raise the boys.

She was a stunning blonde when, at seventeen, she married the budding baseball star. She is still

◄ The Mick, at age 14,
in amateur ball (1945)

▲ Mantle as a rookie in the spring of 1951 opened eyes with his power from both sides of the plate.

◀ Yogi Berra greets Mantle after his titanic home run, 565 feet on the tape measure, against the Senators (1953).

Billy Martin (left) ▶ and Mantle gave Eddie Lopat (center) home run support to beat the Dodgers in the second game of the 1953 World Series.

Casey Stengel ▶
leaves no doubt
that Mickey Mantle
won the American
League's Triple Crown
in 1956.

▲ With a spectacular catch of a drive by Gil Hodges, Mantle saves Don Larsen's perfect game
against the Dodgers in the 1956 World Series.

◀ Mickey poses with Hank Aaron, the player he considered the best of his era, before the 1957 fall classic.

(From left) ▶ Bill Skowron, Roger Maris and Mickey hit two homers each to rout the Red Sox in May of 1961; here they needle Yogi Berra, who had only one.

▲ The Mick and the Giants' Willie Mays discuss good wood before the second game of the 1962 World Series.

◄ A dozen years after their only season as teammates, the regal Joe DiMaggio and Mantle share a moment in the 1963 Yankee camp.

▲ **Number 7's classic follow-through:** Mick homers off Steve Hamilton of the Orioles (1963).

▲ Mantle's 9th-inning home run that beat the Cardinals in Game 3 of the 1964 Series and made a winner of Jim Bouton.

▲ Mickey is congratulated by a young fan after hitting the 500th homer of his career (1967).

▲ Together again: Mick and Whitey Ford recall Yankee glory years on the day of their induction into The Hall of Fame (1974).

stunning—and smart, quick, and well-organized. Merlyn got caught up in the partying herself: "I was doing the same thing as Mick." But she realized she could not keep up with his pace and sought counseling for herself. They loved each other, but the drinking undercut forty-four years of marriage. With one of them sober, one not, they were in different orbits.

I remembered a story about Kyle Rote, another Dallas legend, a football star at SMU and with the New York Giants, divorced from two former Miss Americas. A writer, Dave Klein, went to his apartment in midtown Manhattan to interview him about the historic sudden-death game with the Baltimore Colts. It was in the early afternoon, but Kyle was in his robe.

At one point, the writer asked if he thought he was hard to live with.

Kyle looked around the room, and his gaze took in ashtrays brimming with the stubs of half-smoked cigarettes, cups with rings left by cold coffee, and wastebaskets with newspapers and week-old litter spilling out of them. "You don't see anybody around here, do you?" he asked, a rhetorical question. Kyle gave the room one more sweep and said, "Maybe so, maybe so." Kyle was among the mourners at the church in Dallas.

How easy could it have been living with Mickey Mantle, who had a famous face, and an almost daily golf game that he had to work into his drinking schedule? In spite of the guilt and the doubts that nagged him, his name still meant baseball to the fans who were kids when Mick was sending his homers out to be measured. He could still stop traffic in New York.

No matter what the Cowboys fans may argue, Dallas isn't America. But the ad agencies knew where to find him. It was in the late 1970s that a national survey was taken on how people reacted to the best-known athletes. Stan Musial was the most trusted, with Mantle a close second. Joe Namath was the most recognized, with Mantle right behind him. "It turned out that no matter what question they asked," said Mick, "I was right there at the top."

To Roy True, none of these findings was misleading. Mantle hadn't really tapped his personal appeal during his career, and even his business missteps hadn't raised any character questions. "When Mickey and I first started out together," said True, "everybody told me I ought to make sure Mantle's name was kept before the public or they'd forget him. This didn't make sense to me. How was anybody going to forget Mickey Mantle? Remember, he was essentially a shy and retiring person, a laid-back type of guy. We picked his appearances carefully. Little by little, he became acquainted with the TV medium. He saw when he made a positive impression and when he didn't.

"And it turned out that he was a quick study. When I first got commercials for him, the producers would tell me, 'Better get this guy in a day ahead of time so we can work with him.' I knew this was ridiculous. Mick went in the day of the commercial and in fifteen minutes he had it cold. What's more, he had patience—which you need a lot of when you work with TV and advertising people. I had producers call me later and say, 'Mickey was tremendous. You can't believe the trouble we've had with other jocks.' "

Over the years, Roy was frequently asked to explain Mantle's enduring popularity. "I would tell them," he says, "that it was because Mantle was a legitimate folk hero, a guy from a deprived background, the son of an Oklahoma zinc miner, who made it big in America. But underneath is this basic layer, that he is a regular guy and a good guy. One of the endearing qualities to me about Mickey was simply that he trusted people. He would call me some mornings and say, 'I met a helluva guy last night. A terrific guy. He says he can make me ten million dollars. Will you talk to him?'

"Now that appeals to me, as a lawyer, writing contracts all day that spell out to the last 'T' what anybody can or cannot do—and still you wind up going to court at the end of the hassle. Not with Mickey. For a long time, he didn't doubt anyone's motive if they came at him with a proposition. He thought they were just being nice."

Mantle remained consistent in another way. No matter how great people tried to tell him he was, he didn't take off on ego trips. "He was invited to the White House by President Ford," True recalled, "on the occasion of a visit by the president of France. First of all, he was upset by the fact that he had to wear tails. But most of all, he said, 'I don't understand this deal—why in the world do they want me up there? Do I really have to go?'

"It turned out that he sat at the same table with the president, who made him feel right at home, and Merlyn sat at a table with Nelson Rockefeller, who was extremely gracious to her. When Mickey got back, he called and said, 'Well, you were right. I wouldn't have believed it, but we had the time of our lives.'"

Mickey Mantle. You picture him at nineteen, just up from Joplin, making his first road swing with the Yankees. The first day, he hoarded his money and ate hamburgers and fries at each meal. Then the traveling secretary came through the rail cars, passing out the meal money, ten dollars a day. Mantle didn't know the club paid for their food. It was almost too good to be true. "This is great," he exclaimed. "I ought to be able to save five dollars a day."

When he won the Triple Crown in 1956, the Yankees gave him a raise to $65,000. He recalled with amusement—although it wasn't funny at the time—how the Yankees tried to cut his salary when he did not duplicate those numbers in 1957. He actually hit for a higher average (.365), but his home run production dropped off from 52 to 34.

He signed for a token raise and put the unpleasantness quickly behind him.

He always seemed awed just by where he was, how much he was paid, how people reacted to him. He never fully came to terms with his own success. Pain was his companion, and redemption his destination.

The trend appeared early. In the first game of the World Series of 1951, his rookie season, he blew out his right knee while chasing a short fly ball off the bat of Willie Mays. He pulled up short when he realized DiMaggio was already camped under the ball, and his spikes caught on a sprinkler head.

DiMaggio immediately bent over him, urging him to be still. He had fractured his kneecap and the bone was sticking out of the skin. Joe told him, "They're bringing out a stretcher right now." Mantle joked later that it might have been the most words the great DiMaggio spoke to him that year.

He underwent five knee operations in his eighteen years as a Yankee. In the beginning, he drank because it was part of the baseball culture and to keep up with Whitey Ford and Billy Martin, his fellow midnight travelers. In time, the drinking helped him forget the pain. But he forgot a lot of other things as well, such as where he had been the night before, what he had done, whose wife he might have insulted.

Mantle reached the big leagues at nineteen, all sunny and innocent, a country boy from a town named Commerce in Oklahoma. The beat writers gave him a cornball nickname, the "Commerce Comet," but he never needed it, not with a name like Mickey Mantle. Outside of Babe Ruth, it was probably the best baseball name ever invented. His father picked the name, in honor of Mickey Cochrane, a Hall of Fame catcher for Detroit.

He was eighteen when he signed a Yankee contract in the front seat of scout Tom Greenwade's car. Mantle received a bonus of $1,150 and $400 in salary for the summer.

Later, Greenwade would tell reporters, "I don't quite know how to put this, but when I saw this kid, I knew how Paul Krichell felt the first time he saw Lou Gehrig."

But few legends ever grew from such raw beginnings. In his first spring training start with the Yankees, against Cleveland in Phoenix, he was hit in the face by a high fly ball that broke his sunglasses. "Ray Boone hit the ball," recalled Mantle, "and I wanted a hole in the ground to open up and let me fall in it. I almost got killed by that fly ball. I flipped the glasses down and everything turned completely black. It was the first pair of sunglasses I ever put on.

"The next day Casey said I should stand with one hand like this"—he raised his right hand to his eye—"so I could see the ball and could flip the glasses down. I played the whole game with my hand in the air."

◆   ◆   ◆

He was unschooled, and not very streetwise, but he could amuse you with his down-home wit and touch you when he spoke from his heart.

In Mickey's memory, his father became a sort of superdad, and perhaps he was. Mickey spent his boyhood watching Mutt Mantle play semipro ball on weekends, and the father invested in his oldest son the dreams and ambitions that were never available to him.

In the 1930s, America was a country of miners and farmers and blue-collar workers. Mutt Mantle was a pal to his son in the way fathers of that era needed to be: by working hours that were long and hard to pay the rent and provide the food.

Mick never fared well when he compared himself to his dad, who didn't drink, who spent his nights at home and didn't hang out with the guys. It was the only life the elder Mantle could afford. He wanted more for Mickey, but he could not have imagined how much more the towheaded, doe-eyed kid would enjoy.

Mick didn't push his own sons. The first love of Mickey Jr. was golf, but he had baseball skills he didn't really tap. He signed with the Yankees, giving it up after one year in the low minors. "If *my* father had been *his* father," Mantle said, "Mickey Jr. could have been a big leaguer."

In his mind, Mutt Mantle was always with him. He was in the stands the day Mick blew out his knee in his first World Series in 1951. That same day, Mutt collapsed getting out of the cab, taking his son to Lenox Hill Hospital for knee surgery. They wound up sharing a room. A few days later, Mick learned his father was dying.

He carried the guilt with him through the years because Hodgkin's killed his dad, his grandfather, and two uncles, then skipped him and cut down his son Billy in March 1994. If he hadn't been on the booze, he reasoned, he might have been a more attentive father. He might have kept Billy from getting hooked on alcohol and the prescription drugs that eased the pain of Hodgkin's and caused his heart to fail at thirty-six.

Mantle's career and life were touched and shaped by his drinking and the specter of death, by the memory of his dad and his inheritance of Joe DiMaggio's shoes. He had his demons and his drives.

His relationship with DiMaggio existed mostly in the abstract. To the young Mantle, Joe represented class and elegance and taste, and he never quite got beyond the hero worship he felt for this intensely private man. He probably had not heard of the word "mentor" in 1951. He would have been thrilled if Joe D. had taken him under his wing. But Mantle was too shy to ask for advice, and DiMaggio was too aloof to offer any. Yet his teammates noted that Mick frequently managed to linger near Joe's locker, in case the great one thought of anything he wanted to say.

There was no jealousy between them, just a distance created by the temperament of each. But it was easy for Mickey to feel slighted when Reggie Jackson came along and DiMaggio compared the two of them: "Reggie is a lot like Mantle. They think a 380-foot homer doesn't count. They both tried to hit the ball 500 feet."

DiMaggio did not choose to reveal his likes and dislikes to the public, but the indications are that he wanted Mantle to do well, and in his own way kept track of him. In 1965, with the Yankees suddenly in decline and his injuries taking a toll, Mantle had to be talked out of retirement. He was thirty-four, and the Yankees had no one to replace him.

To further convince Mick that he was needed, the management gave him a "day" in mid-September. They showered him with gifts ranging from a new car and two quarter horses to a Hebrew National salami that was six-feet long and weighed a hundred pounds. Merlyn received a mink coat. Cardinal Spellman was on the planning committee. The music of Guy Lombardo and his Royal Canadians warmed up the crowd.

But nothing was quite as impressive as the presence of DiMaggio, who had flown in from San Francisco to present Mantle to the crowd of fifty thousand. And if he had been upstaged, this was one time Mick would not have minded. DiMaggio, tanned, graying, tailored, looking as he usually did like a member of Parliament, heard the echo of his name and stepped out of the dugout.

Then, seeing Mantle's mother standing to one side, in a gesture unscheduled, he cupped her elbow with his hand and led her to where the players and VIPs were arranged along the infield. When the crowd had calmed down as much as it physically could, DiMaggio said clearly and simply, "I'm proud to introduce the man who succeeded me in centerfield in 1951."

That was a great moment for Mickey, but he

remembered another one, an old-timers' game when there was a slip in protocol. DiMaggio was introduced *ahead* of Mantle, instead of last, as was the custom, and the writers later argued about which player had received the louder or longer ovation. "I heard Joe was pissed off about it," said Mick, grinning as he retold the story.

A year or two later, Mantle was on a radio talk show with Paul Simon, who had written "Mrs. Robinson," the theme for the motion picture *The Graduate.* Simon and Art Garfunkel were the Maris and Mantle of music in the 1960s. The song contained the haunting lyric "Where have you gone, Joe DiMaggio? A nation turns its lonely eyes to you."

During a commercial break, Mickey turned to Paul and asked, "Hey, why didn't you write that line about me?"

What made the question ironic was the fact that Mantle had been Simon's favorite player all during his boyhood. DiMaggio had been his father's hero, and he had taken Paul to Yankee Stadium when he was five to watch Joe play. Simon knew there was something special about the lyrics the moment he wrote them. Even DiMaggio was quoted as saying he was unsure what he felt when he heard the line; but you didn't have to be a baseball fan to be touched by it, and to recognize the lament for a simpler and more romantic time. "They meant," said Simon, "whatever you wanted them to mean."

But he didn't feel he could explain to Mantle all the nuances that went into the song. So he said, "It was the syllables, Mick." Meaning that the phrasing of the lyrics needed the name DiMaggio. Mickey nodded and accepted the answer, as if it made perfect sense to him.

Well, baseball was my whole life. Nothing was ever as much fun as baseball.

—MANTLE, 1988

Over the years, after he had been suckered in a few business deals, booed by the fans, and jabbed in print, Mantle went through periods of being withdrawn, surly, and suspicious. The stories surfaced later about his being rude to kids and ignoring his fans. Part of this was self-protection. For Mantle, it wasn't a matter of dealing with just a small mob of eager, clutching little kids. They came at him in swarms, got underfoot like ants, smeared ice cream on his clothes. The writers were another matter. In New York, as many as fifteen traveled with the team in the 1950s. Mantle reached a point where he could carry on an entire conversation while he dressed after a game, without once lifting his head.

I tricked him into the first interview we ever had. The year was 1965, and the Yankees were scheduled to open Houston's indoor stadium, the Astrodome. During spring training, I stopped by the Yankees' camp in Fort Lauderdale hoping to catch Mantle after a workout. I walked through the stands, toward the field, when I spotted him with two of his teammates heading for the exit. I called out to him, "Mickey! Mickey! Can I get a few minutes with you?"

He didn't turn around, so I climbed over the railing and chased after him. Just before he reached the gate, I made one last plea, using the name of the Texas Christian University coach, and a native Oklahoman: "Darrell Royal asked me to give you a message."

It worked. Mantle stopped in his tracks, turned around, and said, "What's the message?" I said, "Oh, he just told me to say hello if I bumped into you." But that gave me the chance to explain I was with the *Houston Post*, covered the Astros, and needed a few quotes for a story on the opening of the world's first domed stadium.

I didn't stretch the truth too far in hiding behind Royal, a great coach whose Texas teams won three national titles. A few months earlier, Darrell had told me about meeting Mantle, who had been invited by a friend to watch a game between Texas and TCU in Fort Worth.

After the game, the friend suggested they stop by the locker room and say hello to Royal. When the Texas coach shook his hand and said how pleased he was to meet him, Mantle did that little bashful dip of the head and said, "Darrell, we've met before."

The embarrassed Royal said, "We have? When was that?"

"I was a senior in high school" came the reply, "and Bud Wilkinson tried to recruit me to play halfback for Oklahoma. You were the starting quarterback that year. Coach Wilkinson picked you to show me around the campus."

"Oh well," said Royal with a smile of relief, "you weren't Mickey Mantle *then*!"

By 1965, the great years were over for Mantle and for the Yankees too. Johnny Keane had replaced Yogi Berra as the manager in a weird climax to the 1964 World Series, won by the Cardinals. The Yankees were destined to finish sixth, tenth, and ninth in the next three seasons.

There was nothing about the quotes or the story worth recalling, but it paid off when the Yankees showed up for their exhibition series in the Big Bubble. Mantle greeted me politely. In fact, he asked me to settle a rumor that had raced throughout the Yankee clubhouse.

A New York writer heard a rumor that a handsome bachelor on the Houston team had set what was believed to be a major league record, having scored with forty airline hostesses in one month. As the writer understood it, the record had been set during the previous season, and the stud's roommate had kept the official scorecard.

Only one player in the Yankee clubhouse thought such an athletic feat was even possible. That was Mantle, and he thought Joe Pepitone could do it.

"Me? Hell no, Mick," said Pepitone, with a vigorous shake of his head. "That's more than one a night. That's incredible. The best month I ever had was twenty."

"Aw, Joe, you could do it," said Mick proudly, "if you went downtown and really worked at it."

To a man, the Yankees were pleased and relieved to learn that the record had been achieved over the course of one year, not one month. Even so, the Yankees agreed the record was impressive, if you considered time lost to travel, injuries, and monogamous relationships that might last for weeks.

The Yankees had begun their slide into futility, and the quality of the discussions in the clubhouse did not show any significant improvement. Whitey Ford retired first and went on the road as a traveling pitching coach. Mantle was miserable, taking his meals in his room, having no one to run with, knowing his skills had declined, feeling himself overtaken by time at thirty-five.

◆   ◆   ◆

*I can't hit when I need to. I can't steal a base when I
    want to. I can't go from first to third when I have
    to. It was time to quit trying.*
—MANTLE, EXPLAINING HIS DECISION TO RETIRE
AFTER THE 1968 SEASON

Over the years, I bumped into Mantle in Dallas
or Houston, wrote my quota of columns about him
and a story or two for a national magazine. I wrote
one on an occasion Mick never thought he would
observe. The headline on the story was MICKEY
MANTLE IS, GULP, 50!"

It turned out he still had dreams about baseball,
about playing again, a sign of how hard it was for
him to let go of what had been his finest moments.
"I still have them," he said, "the same dreams.
Nearly every night. There's the one where I'm
making a comeback. I get a base hit and I run to
first, hard as I can, but I can't make it. They always
just nick me as I cross the bag.

"But this is the worst one: I get to the ballpark late, and as I jump out of the cab, I hear them calling my name on the public address system. I try to get in and all the gates are locked. Then I see a hole under a fence and I can see Casey looking for me, all of 'em, Billy and Whitey and Yogi. I try to crawl through the hole and I get stuck at the hips, and that's when I wake up, sweating."

This was in 1982 and Stengel had been dead for fifteen years; no, Mickey wasn't surprised that he had outlived Casey. Yogi Berra was back with the Yankees as a coach, and a year later Billy Martin would rejoin them as the new manager. Whitey Ford had been inducted into the Hall of Fame with Mantle in 1974.

Mantle, Martin, and Ford —these were the three who seemed to refuse to grow older.

Mickey had just about quit going to the games. When he did, he sat in one of those VIP boxes where they serve little sausages on a toothpick.

The fans would never let him enjoy the game otherwise. He wouldn't, anyway. He never got used to not playing.

He didn't enjoy the dreams, either: "Hell no, I keep getting thrown out." But they were a source of entertainment, home movies of the subconscious mind. "I met a guy in a bar one night"—this was a time when Mick started a lot of his sentences with those words—"and he said he was, what do you call them, an analyst. He told me he could explain what my dreams meant, so I described the one about me trying to crawl under the fence.

"He spun around on his seat and said, 'My God, that's terrible! You must have been late to a lot of games.' Well, I thought about that. The truth is, I missed a lot of buses, maybe a plane or two. Had to catch cabs. But I was *never* late for a game."

Looking back, from the sad vantage point of August 1995, at the ending of a famous life, we know exactly what Darrell Royal meant. Except for baseball, being Mickey Mantle was just about the only job he had. He was a coach for the Yankees one season under Ralph Houk, but he knew he wasn't cut out for it when Bobby Murcer walked to lead off an inning, turned to Mantle, and asked, "What's the sign?"

"I don't know about yours," said Mick, "but I'm a Libra."

He spent that one season as a coach and another as a TV analyst on NBC, and he quit both jobs because he felt as if he was stealing their money. And Mickey Charles Mantle never cheated anyone in his life, with the possible exception of himself.

I could never be a manager. I can't manage myself. What would I do with twenty-five other problems?
—MANTLE, IN MULTIPLE INTERVIEWS

Mantle had an interesting way of joining a conversation, taking one position, and working his way to the other side. He maintained in virtually all of his public utterances that he had no desire to manage a ball club.

But after some reflection, he hinted that it would have been nice if an owner had asked. "It might have helped me shape up," he said. "I might have taken it seriously, stopped drinking, and found out if I could do the job, and if I liked it."

Then the word slips out that Mantle was, in fact, considered for the manager's job with the Texas Rangers, when owner Bob Short moved the team from Washington, D.C. The approach was made in a roundabout way, and if an offer was in the works it got scuttled by rumors that Mickey was hustling bets at Preston Trail, a tightly knit, all-male Dallas golf club of two hundred members. He felt the bite of that memory for years. "Lordy," he said, "if anything it was the other way around. I always accused the guys I played with of hustling me. That's what the first tee is all about."

Short did telephone and invited Mantle to meet him for an early breakfast. In spite of his reservations, he felt a surge of excitement. The country-cooking franchises were in the pits, and his cash flow had been reduced to a trickle, at least for the short term. This was room service: a new franchise, in a city he called home, with a ballpark twenty minutes from his door. He confided his hopes to Merlyn. "Mickey, that sounds great," she said. "I know you'll make a good manager."

After the initial chitchat, Short cut right to the point: "I need to hire a manager, and I wondered if you had anyone you want to recommend."

If Short had toyed with the Mantle name and image, the notion clearly had been sidetracked. Mick urged him to hire Billy Martin, took a bite of toast and a swallow of coffee, and left the rest of his breakfast on the table.

Under Martin, the Rangers enjoyed their first pennant race in 1974 and finished second. Billy was fired in 1975.

How Mantle might have fared as a manager is anyone's guess. But when you consider that the team's first skipper was Ted Williams, you have to believe the Rangers would not have suffered from a low profile. They lost one hundred games under Williams, who then retired to his favorite fishing holes in Florida.

Perhaps twice in his sixty-three years, Mickey Mantle was not treated as a celebrity, certainly not an icon. For the first eighteen, he was mostly Mutt Mantle's boy. He grew up dirt-poor but lucky, because his father recognized that baseball was his son's ticket out of the zinc mines.

The other time was more recent—January 1994. When Mick checked himself into The Betty Ford Center in California to deal with his addiction to alcohol, his identity didn't matter. He was simply "the fellow in Room 202." The adjustment was no walk in the park, but it was refreshing for a change not to be Mickey Mantle.

"We had jobs," he said. "One of mine was to get up at five forty-five and wake up everyone else in my dormitory. Later, I cleared the dishes after lunch. I kind of enjoyed that."

Most of what the public heard or read about Mantle was encouraging. He made the tour to promote his book, he showed up at celebrity golf tournaments, and held his fantasy baseball camps. He felt ten years younger, he said, and he was thrilled by the letters he received. They made him feel useful. He was helping people with their drinking problems just by talking about his own.

And no one can know how much pride had to be choked down, when you are Mickey Mantle and it is time to admit that your troubles are real, and you can't make them go away by ignoring or denying them.

There is no record of how many baseball players have gone from the Hall of Fame to working as a busboy, but for Mantle there was no confusion. Until his final plague of ailments, the liver transplant and the cancer, he had a freshness about him and a modesty that can't be faked. And even as the lines deepened and the flesh began to sag, the face was open and earnest, the kind you can see on any Little League field in America. The freckled, blue-eyed southwestern face had become a type.

He was so much a man-child himself, it was all the more unsettling when he was rude or sulky with kids. The drinking and the pain in his knees made him cranky and impatient. "I can remember ten or twelve times pushing away kids who wanted autographs," he said. "Then I'd get on a plane, order a drink, and sit there feeling guilty the rest of the flight."

This was a pattern familiar to his friends. He tried to get around it by keeping a stash of the presigned cards in his pocket, and he passed them out when he was rushing through an airport or trying to leave a hotel or a restaurant.

But he made a lot of phone calls for strangers who knew a little boy who was gravely ill, and he didn't take any bows for those. He could floor you with glimpses of a sweet innocence that bordered on the naïve.

When he sat in a car for more than fifteen minutes, his legs sometimes stiffened and he needed help getting out. He hated for anyone to see him like that, but he was not the kind of athlete who studied himself in a mirror, checking out his image.

Once, he paid a visit to Disneyland and posed for photographs with several of the famous Disney characters, Mickey and Minnie and the gang. They lined him up in the middle of the shot. The photographer glanced up from his camera and motioned with his hand: "Goofy, move a little to the right, please."

Obligingly, Mantle leaned his head and shoulder over a few inches.

"Uh, I didn't mean you, Mr. Mantle," the flustered photographer said. "I was talking to the guy directly behind you." Mick looked up, and there was Goofy, eight feet tall with long, furry ears.

Asked if he thought some joker with a camera was really likely to address him as "Goofy," Mantle shrugged and said, "I've been called worse."

There is no need to belabor the point, but death was no stranger to Mantle. He feared it when he was in his teens and twenties, back when he didn't expect to reach forty. Later, in a curious way, it became a kind of competition for him. When Vic Raschi died during the year I helped Mick write his book, he said, "Man, I never thought I'd outlive Vic Raschi." He said the same thing, at different times, about Elston Howard and about Don Larsen, whose drinking habits were far better known than Mantle's. He said it when he talked about his wild and hotheaded friend Billy Martin, and again when he heard the news that Don Drysdale, the great Dodger pitcher, had died in his hotel room of a

heart attack. "I never thought I'd outlive Drysdale."
It was as if he woke up every morning, from forty
on, surprised to find himself still alive.

This condition did not necessarily translate into
happiness, but Mick was never the burdened, tor-
mented soul he seemed to be when people looked
at the end of his life through the small end of the
telescope.

Hard-core baseball fans, and even casual stu-
dents of human behavior, wondered how Mickey
Mantle, who had soaked up so much glory and
adulation, could be so self-destructive. How could
he drink steadily for forty years and not know, or
deny, that he was an alcoholic?

The answer isn't pretty. You had to understand
the baseball culture that Mantle embraced. In the
clubhouse, the equipment man kept the beer iced
down in washtubs. The players would knock back
four or five before they left the stadium for a night
on the town.

It was such a macho time and place that Mantle

didn't think beer and wine counted as real drink-ing. Most athletes didn't. Anyway, no one was keeping score.

I never knew how someone who was dying could say he was the luckiest man in the world. But now I understand.

—MANTLE, ON THE DAY HIS NUMBER 7 WAS RETIRED AT YANKEE STADIUM, IN JUNE 1969, REFERRING TO LOU GEHRIG'S FAREWELL SPEECH

The news, in June 1995, that he needed a liver transplant, seemed almost cruel and mocking. He could no longer guard his shyness, his secrets, his hurts, his regrets. The son of an Oklahoma miner, who hated hospitals, would spend his last innings in one.

Mantle's liver was diseased from cancer and years of alcohol abuse. His case was complicated by the presence of hepatitis C, probably from a blood transfusion, the doctors judged, related to one of the surgeries during his baseball career. Mantle was described as a model patient, despite the indignity of having his anatomy explained by pie charts and graphs on television and newsprint.

He underwent what was described as life-saving surgery on June 8, 1995. The next day a second operation was needed to stem the bleeding around the transplanted liver. On the tenth he was removed from intensive care and on the eleventh he got out of bed and walked a few steps to a chair.

On June 22, the doctors treated him with steroids, a move designed to counter the signs of a slight organ rejection. On the twenty-third, Mantle received chemotherapy, and was scheduled to undergo more treatments over the next four to six months to combat his hepatoma, "a potentially aggressive" liver cancer.

He was discharged from the hospital on June 28 and moved into the home of his son Danny. Charts and diagrams appeared in newspapers across the land. In this kind of case, sources said, the patient might have eighteen months to five years of additional, active life. Television viewers saw Mantle in a weak but chipper mood in his July 11 press conference, less so in a brief, second statement. He looked gaunt and shrunken as he revealed that the cancer had been detected in his lungs. The news had been fairly hopeful up to that day. He had returned to the hospital complaining of more pain in his abdomen. The cancer spread quickly throughout his body.

There was talk of more chemotherapy, but one day's headlines were contradicted by the next. Meanwhile, Mantle knew. The doctors had told him that his condition could not be treated; all they could do was make him comfortable. One of his physicians said, "In terms of time—" Mantle cut him off sharply. "I don't want to know," he said.

He was caught in a dreadful catch-22. The drugs that were intended to help his body fight off the rejection of his new liver did so by feeding the tissue and cells.

"This is the most aggressive cancer that anyone on the medical team has ever seen," said Dr. Goran Klintman of the Baylor University Medical Center.

He was visited at midweek by some of his former New York Yankee teammates, including Whitey Ford, Bobby Richardson, Hank Bauer, and Moose Skowron. "I think that Mickey was ready to go," said Dr. Daniel DeMarco, his gastroenterologist. "At one point he asked, 'What are we waiting for?'"

Sedated with morphine, he was in and out of consciousness his last forty-eight hours. He was awake for the last time just after midnight, saw Merlyn and David, held their hands, and lapsed back into sleep. "He was never in pain," Dr. DeMarco said.

By contrast, Mantle had been rarely without pain through virtually his entire baseball career.

His legacy was expected to be the deeds he performed on one leg, his tape-measure home runs, and his World Series rings. But in his restless search for a purpose beyond baseball, something he could classify as important, and meaningful, Mantle may have found his permanent legacy in his final months and days.

There was the renewed closeness to his family, to Merlyn, Mickey Jr., David, and Danny, all of them having dealt with their dependencies, sober and pulling together. The love of a family isn't unusual, but getting the roles right, unloading the guilt and other excess baggage, was a big hit for the Mantles.

"I never felt I was there for them when they were growing up," said Mick. "When they were old enough, we became drinking buddies. It kind of felt like the old days with Billy and Whitey."

He didn't pressure them to improve their grades or stay in school. He didn't find the time to encourage whatever talents they had, or play catch or haul them off to their own games.

"We understood," said Mickey Jr. "His job kept him away for six months. He was a great dad. We were proud of him, proud of being his sons."

But a clearheaded Mantle had to revisit his relationships. "When I realized what I had done to my sons," he said, "it just tore me up. I thought, 'My God, what have I done?' " He said it in the tone of voice Alec Guinness used in the movie *The Bridge on the River Kwai* when it dawns on him that he has helped the Japanese enemy build a bridge to be used against the Allied forces.

He couldn't undo the past, but in the time he had left Mantle became a father in action as well as name. "We talked about things I never imagined we would talk about," said Danny. "I didn't really get to spend much time with him until I was sixteen. We went out and had beers."

Even before he knew the clock was running out on him, the Mickey Mantle Foundation had been established. Mick had intended to fill the role of a national spokesman for the organ donor program which, oh so briefly, he believed had extended his life. His program will go forward under the label of "Mickey's Team" and use a slogan he coined: "Be a hero, be a donor." Saving lives, the family hopes, will turn out to be Mick's true legacy.

And as he had on so many sunny days for the Yankees of the 1950s and 1960s, Mantle drew one more standing-room-only crowd. This one was at the Lovers Lane United Methodist Church, where one thousand mourners filled the pews, and at least that many more milled around outside, listening to the service on loudspeakers. Some had spent the night, sleeping on the lawn, in order to pay their last respects to a fragile hero—in the phrase of Bob Costas—who became an American icon. That is a mighty fancy word, "icon," for a fellow as plainspoken as Mantle. But he was indeed one of a kind, one for his time.

An Appreciation

He was my childhood.

—ACTOR-COMEDIAN BILLY CRYSTAL, EXPLAINING
WHY HE HAD FLOWN FROM NEW YORK TO
DALLAS TO ATTEND MANTLE'S FUNERAL

He faced death bravely, with dignity, but no one really expected him to do otherwise. The depth of his fame may be based in part on his link to the 1950s, a decade that passed in the shadow of a mushroom cloud, but gave us simpler pleasures: Elvis, penny loafers, Hula Hoops, I Like Ike, *American Bandstand,* Edward R. Murrow, McCarthyism, rock 'n' roll, *Sputnik,* and *The $64,000 Question.*

Or it may have been something called charisma: Mantle, with the lopsided grin and the broad back and the tape-measure home run. And then there is Mantle as he would have been scripted by Shakespeare, trying to outrun what he believed was a family curse.

There is no point in harping anymore on what he might have accomplished on sound wheels.

When he hit his five hundredth home run, only five other players had preceded him, and their names are Babe Ruth, Willie Mays, Jimmy Foxx, Ted Williams, and Mel Ott.

His Yankee teammates filled most of a pew at the church, and his pallbearers included two Hall of Famers—Yogi Berra and Whitey Ford, who was inducted with Mantle in 1974.

In a flawless eulogy, Bob Costas, the NBC sportscaster, who has carried Mantle's rookie card in his billfold since childhood, said he was there to represent the millions of kids "who grew up in the fifties and sixties and for whom Mickey Mantle was baseball.

"And more than that he was a presence in our lives—a fragile hero to whom we had an emotional attachment so strong and lasting that it defied logic. . . . He was the most compelling baseball hero of our lifetime. And he was our symbol of baseball at a time when the game meant something to us that perhaps it no longer does. . . .

"In the end, people got it. And Mantle got from America something other than misplaced and mindless celebrity worship. . . . He got love—love for what he had been, love for what he made us feel, love for the humanity and sweetness that was always there mixed in with the flaws and all the pain that racked his body and his soul. . . .

"And our last memories of Mickey Mantle are as heroic as the first. . . ."

Bobby Richardson, the former second baseman and now a lay minister, had prayed with Mick in the hospital, and he held his hand when Mantle whispered that he had found his God. It did not seem at all a contradiction when Bobby recalled Mantle's brand of clubhouse humor: hiding a snake in a teammate's slacks, egging on Phil Linz into a confrontation with the usually mild Yogi Berra, then the Yankees' manager.

Linz decided to practice on a new harmonica in the back of the bus, while Berra, upset by a narrow loss, was fuming in a front seat. The only selection Linz knew at that stage of his de-velopment was "Mary Had a Little Lamb," not a pop favorite even in the mid-sixties. When he could tolerate it no more, Yogi stood up and, over the noise of the motor, shouted toward the rear of the bus, "Take that thing and shove it up your..."

Linz looked over to Mantle and asked, "I missed that. What did Yogi say?"

Mick leaned across the aisle. "He said he can't hear you up front, and to play it again, louder," which he did. Berra rushed the length of the bus and screamed in Phil's face that he would be hit with a stiff fine. It worked out well in the end. Yogi was able to establish a bit more authority over the team, and Linz wound up getting a commercial for a company that sold harmonicas.

After a fairly strong dosage of laughter and tears, Roy Clark kept a promise he had made years ago, "but still way too soon." He sang a song that was Mantle's favorite, the lyrics fitting so closely the tempo of his days, "Yesterday When I Was Young."

The contradictions were still there on the day Mantle drew his last capacity crowd. The memories of the airy, vibrant Mick outweighed the sadness. He had said that week, and many times before, how he wanted to be remembered: as a good teammate. In that respect, he overachieved. "What can you say," asked Gene Woodling, "after you have said how great he was?" It was fun being Mickey Mantle, but it wasn't easy. There was mischief in him, but no meanness. He was the home run hitter who could beat out infield hits, the country hick who conquered New York, the fearless soul who made fun of his own mortality.

Yogi made me promise him that we would go to each other's funerals. He was afraid I wouldn't go to his.

—MANTLE, JULY 1995

Costas recealled how the kids of his generation wanted to walk and talk like Mickey. Billy Crystal said he recited his bar mitzvah service in an Oklahoma drawl.

Between Bob Costas and Roy Clark, white handkerchiefs began popping out of pockets up and down the pews, so that the effect was similar to a crowd doing the wave at a sports event.

I did get the answer to the question that had lingered in my mind since Fort Lauderdale.

Three times while he was in the intensive care unit, Mickey Mantle stirred himself awake, and finding his sons at his bedside, repeated the words, "I love you."